Best-Loved Pies

Publications International, Ltd.

Pictured on the front cover: Plum & Walnut Pie *(page 98).*

Pictured on the back cover *(clockwise from top left):* Southern Oatmeal Pie *(page 10),* Carnation® Key Lime Pie *(page 122)* and Chocolate Chess Pie *(page 8).*

Microwave Cooking: Microwave ovens vary in wattage. Use the cooking times as guidelines and check for doneness before adding more time.

Preparation/Cooking Times: Preparation times are based on the approximate amount of time required to assemble the recipe before cooking, baking, chilling or serving. These times include preparation steps such as measuring, chopping and mixing. The fact that some preparations and cooking can be done simultaneously is taken into account. Preparation of optional ingredients and serving suggestions is not included.

Publications International, Ltd.

Table of Contents

banana cream pie

1 unbaked 9-inch pie crust
3 bananas, divided
1 teaspoon lemon juice
$\frac{1}{2}$ cup sugar
6 tablespoons cornstarch
$\frac{1}{4}$ teaspoon salt
3 cups milk
2 egg yolks
$1\frac{1}{2}$ teaspoons vanilla
Whipped cream (optional)
Ground cinnamon (optional)

1. Preheat oven to 400°F. Prick holes in bottom of crust with fork. Bake 10 minutes or until lightly browned. Cool 15 minutes on wire rack.

2. Slice 2 bananas; toss with lemon juice. Layer on bottom of crust.

3. Combine sugar, cornstarch and salt in medium saucepan. Combine milk and egg yolks in medium bowl; slowly stir into sugar mixture. Cook and stir over medium heat until thickened. Boil 1 minute, stirring constantly. Remove from heat; stir in vanilla. Pour into crust; immediately cover with waxed paper. Refrigerate 2 hours or until ready to serve.

4. Remove waxed paper and slice remaining banana. Arrange slices around edge of pie. Garnish with whipped cream and cinnamon.

Makes 8 servings

fried apple-cranberry pies

1 package (about 15 ounces) refrigerated pie crusts
3 tablespoons unsalted butter
3 Gala apples (about 12 ounces), peeled and diced
3 tablespoons dried cranberries
3 tablespoons packed brown sugar
1½ tablespoons lemon juice
¾ teaspoon ground cinnamon
¼ teaspoon ground nutmeg
Pinch salt
Vegetable oil
Powdered sugar

1. Let crusts stand at room temperature 15 minutes. Melt butter in large skillet over medium heat. Add apples; cook 8 minutes, stirring frequently. Add cranberries, brown sugar, lemon juice, cinnamon, nutmeg and salt; cook and stir 4 minutes or until apples are tender. Transfer to medium bowl; cool 15 minutes.

2. Heat 2 cups oil in 12-inch skillet over medium heat to 350°F.

3. Roll out each crust into 12½-inch circle on floured surface; cut out seven 4-inch circles. Place generous tablespoon of apple mixture on half of one dough circle, leaving ¼-inch border. Dip finger in water and moisten edge. Fold dough over filling, pressing lightly. Dip fork in flour and crimp edge of dough to seal completely. Repeat with remaining dough and filling.

4. Working in three batches, fry pies 1 minute. Turn and fry 1 minute or until lightly browned. Transfer pies to paper-towel lined baking pan. Allow oil temperature to return to 350°F between batches.

5. Sprinkle with powdered sugar just before serving.   *Makes 14 pies*

Variation: These pies can also be baked on a baking sheet in a preheated 425°F oven for 10 minutes or until lightly browned.

fried apple-cranberry pies

chocolate chess pie

4 squares (1 ounce each) unsweetened chocolate
3 tablespoons unsalted butter
3 eggs
1 egg yolk
1¼ cups sugar
½ cup half-and-half
1 to 2 teaspoons instant coffee granules
¼ teaspoon salt
1 unbaked 9-inch pie crust
   Whipped cream
   Chocolate-covered coffee beans (optional)

1. Preheat oven to 325°F. Cook and stir chocolate and butter in small heavy saucepan over low heat until melted. Let stand 15 minutes.

2. Whisk eggs and egg yolk in medium bowl. Whisk in sugar, half-and-half, coffee granules and salt until blended. Whisk in chocolate mixture until smooth. Pour into crust.

3. Bake 35 minutes or until set. Cool completely on wire rack.

4. Refrigerate 2 hours or until ready to serve. Serve with whipped cream. Garnish with chocolate-covered coffee beans.   *Makes 8 servings*

Note: Use 2 teaspoons instant coffee granules for a more pronounced coffee flavor.

chocolate chess pie

southern oatmeal pie

½ (about 15-ounce) package refrigerated pie crusts
4 eggs
1 cup light corn syrup
½ cup packed brown sugar
6 tablespoons unsalted butter, melted and cooled
1½ teaspoons vanilla
½ teaspoon salt
1 cup quick oats
Whipped cream and sliced plums (optional)

1. Let crust stand at room temperature 15 minutes. Preheat oven to 375°F. Line 9-inch pie plate with crust; flute edge.

2. Whisk eggs in medium bowl. Whisk in corn syrup, brown sugar, butter, vanilla and salt until well blended. Stir in oats. Pour into crust.

3. Bake 35 minutes or until edge is set. Cool 30 minutes on wire rack.

4. Serve warm or at room temperature with whipped cream and sliced plums, if desired.   *Makes 8 servings*

TIP According to popular folklore, the oatmeal pie first became popular during the Civil War. Wartime shortages of pecans across the southern part of the country led to this ingenious substitution. The nuttiness and chewiness of the oats highlights the same brown sugar and vanilla flavors found in traditional pecan pie.

southern oatmeal pie

sweet potato pie

3 large sweet potatoes, peeled and cut into cubes (about 3 cups)
$\frac{1}{4}$ cup heavy cream
1 can (10$\frac{3}{4}$ ounces) CAMPBELL'S® Condensed Tomato Soup
1 cup packed brown sugar
3 eggs
1 teaspoon vanilla extract
$\frac{1}{2}$ teaspoon ground cinnamon
$\frac{1}{2}$ teaspoon ground nutmeg
1 (9-inch) frozen pie crust

1. Heat the oven to 350°F.

2. Place potatoes into a 3-quart saucepan and add water to cover. Heat over medium-high heat to a boil. Reduce the heat to low. Cover and cook for 10 minutes or until the potatoes are tender. Drain the potatoes well in a colander.

3. Place the potatoes and heavy cream into a large bowl. Beat with an electric mixer on medium speed until the mixture is fluffy. Beat in the soup, brown sugar, eggs, vanilla extract, cinnamon and nutmeg. Pour the potato mixture into the pie crust and place onto a baking sheet.

4. Bake for 1 hour or until set. Cool the pie in the pan on a wire rack about 3 hours.

Makes 8 servings

Kitchen Tip: Substitute 1$\frac{3}{4}$ cups drained and mashed canned sweet potatoes for the fresh mashed sweet potatoes.

Prep Time: 15 minutes | Bake Time: 1 hour | Cool Time: 3 hours

sweet potato pie

chocolate caramel surprise pie

1½ cups plus 6 tablespoons whipping cream, divided
8 ounces semisweet chocolate, chopped, divided
1 (6-ounce) chocolate crumb pie crust
¼ cup caramel dessert topping
6 tablespoons sugar, divided
¼ teaspoon salt
3 egg yolks
½ teaspoon vanilla
   Whipped topping and caramels (optional)

1. Cook and stir ½ cup cream and 4 ounces semisweet chocolate in small heavy saucepan over low heat until chocolate is melted; cool slightly. Spread evenly in crust. Refrigerate 30 minutes.

2. Spread dessert topping over chocolate. Refrigerate 30 minutes.

3. Cook and stir 1 cup cream and remaining 4 ounces semisweet chocolate in same saucepan over low heat until chocolate is melted. Stir in 4 tablespoons sugar and salt; cool slightly.

4. Whisk egg yolks in small bowl. Pour ½ cup chocolate mixture into egg yolks, whisking constantly. Pour egg mixture back into saucepan; cook and stir over low heat until mixture is thickened. Cook 1 minute. (Mixture should reach 160°F on instant-read thermometer.) Transfer to large bowl; stir in vanilla. Refrigerate 30 minutes, stirring occasionally.

5. Beat remaining 6 tablespoons cream and 2 tablespoons sugar in small bowl with electric mixer at high speed until stiff peaks form. Fold whipped cream into chocolate mixture. Gently spoon over caramel layer. Refrigerate 4 hours or overnight. Serve with whipped topping and caramels, if desired. *Makes 10 servings*

chocolate caramel surprise pie

apple pie with cheddar streusel

Cheddar Streusel (recipe follows)
8 cups sliced peeled apples (Rome Beauty, Fuji or Northern Spy)
$\frac{1}{2}$ cup packed dark brown sugar
$\frac{1}{3}$ cup granulated sugar
3 tablespoons all-purpose flour
$\frac{1}{2}$ teaspoon ground cinnamon
$\frac{1}{4}$ teaspoon salt
Single-Crust Pie Pastry (recipe follows)
1 cup (4 ounces) shredded sharp Cheddar cheese, divided

1. Prepare Cheddar Streusel. Preheat oven to 425°F.

2. Place apples in large bowl. Add brown sugar, granulated sugar, flour, cinnamon and salt; toss to coat.

3. Roll out pastry into 11-inch circle on floured surface. Sprinkle with $\frac{1}{2}$ cup cheese; roll lightly to adhere. Line 9-inch pie pan with pastry; flute edge.

4. Spoon filling into crust, packing down. Sprinkle with Cheddar Streusel. Place pie on rimmed baking sheet.

5. Bake 15 minutes. *Reduce oven temperature to 350°F.* Lightly tent pie with foil; bake 35 minutes. Remove foil; sprinkle with remaining $\frac{1}{2}$ cup cheese. Bake 10 minutes or until cheese is melted and crust is golden brown. Cool 30 minutes before slicing. *Makes 8 servings*

Cheddar Streusel: Combine $\frac{1}{3}$ cup all-purpose flour, $\frac{1}{3}$ cup granulated sugar, $\frac{1}{3}$ cup packed dark brown sugar and $\frac{1}{4}$ teaspoon salt in medium bowl. Cut in 5 tablespoons cubed unsalted butter with pastry blender or two knives until mixture resembles coarse crumbs.

Single-Crust Pie Pastry: Combine $1\frac{1}{4}$ cups flour and $\frac{1}{2}$ teaspoon salt in medium bowl. Cut in 3 tablespoons shortening and 3 tablespoons cubed unsalted butter with pastry blender or two knives until mixture resembles coarse crumbs. Combine 3 tablespoons water and $\frac{1}{2}$ teaspoon cider vinegar in small bowl. Add to flour mixture; mix with fork until dough forms, adding additional water as needed. Form dough into disc; wrap in plastic wrap. Refrigerate 30 minutes.

butter pecan pie

1 cup coarsely chopped pecans
1/4 cup butter or margarine
1 container DUNCAN HINES® Creamy Home-Style Buttercream
　　Frosting
1 package (8 ounces) cream cheese, softened
1 cup frozen non-dairy whipped topping, thawed
1 (9-inch) graham cracker pie crust
　　Pecan halves for garnish

1. Place pecans and butter in 10-inch skillet on medium heat. Cook, stirring constantly, until butter is lightly browned. Pour into heatproof large bowl. Add frosting and cream cheese. Stir until thoroughly blended.

2. Fold in whipped topping. Pour into crust. Garnish with pecan halves, if desired. Refrigerate for 4 hours or until firm. *Makes 8 servings*

mom's pumpkin pie

1½ cans (15 ounces each) solid-pack pumpkin
1 can (12 ounces) evaporated milk
1 cup sugar
2 eggs
2 tablespoons maple syrup
1 teaspoon ground cinnamon
1 teaspoon vanilla
1/2 teaspoon salt
2 unbaked 9-inch pie crusts
　　Whipped cream (optional)

1. Preheat oven to 350°F. Combine pumpkin, evaporated milk, sugar, eggs, maple syrup, cinnamon, vanilla and salt in large bowl. Spread evenly in crusts.

2. Place pies on baking sheet. Bake 1 hour or until knife inserted into centers comes out clean. Cool completely on wire rack. Serve with whipped cream, if desired. *Makes 16 servings*

caribbean coconut pie

1 unbaked deep-dish 9-inch pie crust
1 can (14 ounces) sweetened condensed milk
¾ cup flaked coconut
2 eggs
½ cup hot water
2 teaspoons grated lime peel
   Juice of 1 lime
¼ teaspoon salt
⅛ teaspoon ground red pepper
   Whipped cream (optional)

1. Preheat oven to 400°F. Prick holes in bottom of crust with fork. Bake 10 minutes or until lightly browned. Cool 15 minutes on wire rack.

2. *Reduce oven temperature to 350°F.* Combine sweetened condensed milk, coconut, eggs, water, lime peel, lime juice, salt and red pepper in large bowl. Pour into crust.

3. Bake 30 minutes or until knife inserted into center comes out clean. Cool completely on wire rack.

4. Serve with whipped cream, if desired. Store leftovers covered in refrigerator.   *Makes 8 servings*

caribbean coconut pie

fancy fudge pie

1 cup chocolate wafer crumbs
⅓ cup butter, melted
1⅓ cups (8 ounces) semisweet chocolate chips
¾ cup packed brown sugar
½ cup (1 stick) butter, softened
3 eggs
1 cup chopped pecans
½ cup all-purpose flour
1 teaspoon vanilla
½ teaspoon instant espresso powder
    Whipped cream (optional)
    Chocolate syrup (optional)

1. Preheat oven to 375°F. Combine wafer crumbs and melted butter in small bowl. Press onto bottom and up side of 9-inch pie pan. Bake 5 minutes. Cool completely on wire rack.

2. Place chocolate chips in small microwavable bowl. Microwave on HIGH 1 minute or until melted and smooth. Cool slightly.

3. Beat brown sugar and softened butter in large bowl with electric mixer at medium speed until light and fluffy. Add eggs, one at a time, beating well after each addition. Stir in chocolate, pecans, flour, vanilla and espresso powder. Pour into crust.

4. Bake 30 minutes or until set. Cool completely on wire rack. Cover and refrigerate 2 hours or until ready to serve. Garnish with whipped cream and chocolate syrup. *Makes 8 servings*

sour cream squash pie

   1 package (12 ounces) frozen winter squash, thawed and drained
 1/2 cup sour cream
 1/4 cup sugar
   1 egg
1 1/2 teaspoons pumpkin pie spice
 1/2 teaspoon salt
 1/2 teaspoon vanilla
 3/4 cup evaporated milk
   1 (6-ounce) graham cracker pie crust
 1/4 cup chopped hazelnuts, toasted (optional)

1. Preheat oven to 350°F. Whisk squash, sour cream, sugar, egg, pumpkin pie spice, salt and vanilla in large bowl. Whisk in evaporated milk. Pour into crust.

2. Bake 1 hour 10 minutes or until set. Cool completely on wire rack. Sprinkle with hazelnuts just before serving, if desired.   *Makes 8 servings*

TIP The addition of sour cream in this delicious pie serves two purposes. The creamy texture helps to smooth out the graininess that squash alone can sometimes have, while the subtle tartness creates a pleasant contrast with the sweetness of the other ingredients.

sour cream squash pie

kansas city mud pie

1¼ cups finely chopped PLANTERS® Pecans
¾ cup all-purpose flour
¼ cup (½ stick) butter or margarine, melted
2 packages (8 ounces each) PHILADELPHIA® Cream Cheese, softened
1½ cups sifted powdered sugar
1 tub (8 ounces) COOL WHIP® Whipped Topping, thawed, divided
2⅔ cups cold milk
2 packages (4-serving size each) JELL-O® Chocolate Flavor Instant Pudding & Pie Filling

HEAT oven to 375°F. Mix pecans, flour and butter; press onto bottom of 9-inch springform pan. Bake 20 minutes. Cool.

BEAT cream cheese and sugar with electric mixer until well blended. Gently stir in 1½ cups of the whipped topping; spread over crust. Beat milk and dry pudding mixes with wire whisk 2 minutes or until well blended. Spoon over cream cheese layer.

REFRIGERATE several hours or until set. Run knife or metal spatula around rim of pan to loosen dessert; remove rim. Top pie with remaining whipped topping just before serving. Store leftovers in refrigerator.

Makes 16 servings

Jazz It Up: Drizzle each serving plate with 1 tablespoon raspberry sauce before topping with pie slice.

Prep Time: 30 minutes

kansas city mud pie

buttermilk pie

1½ cups sugar
1 tablespoon cornstarch
3 eggs
½ cup buttermilk
¼ cup (½ stick) butter, melted and cooled
1 tablespoon lemon juice
1 teaspoon vanilla
1 (6-ounce) graham cracker pie crust
Whipped cream (optional)

1. Preheat oven to 350°F. Combine sugar and cornstarch in medium bowl. Beat in eggs, buttermilk, butter, lemon juice and vanilla with electric mixer at medium speed until smooth. Pour into crust.

2. Bake 40 minutes or until set. Cool completely on wire rack.

3. Refrigerate 2 hours or until ready to serve. Serve with whipped cream, if desired. *Makes 8 servings*

TIP Buttermilk is the main flavoring agent in this classic pie, however, it can be difficult to find in some small grocery stores. In a pinch, you may substitute powdered buttermilk, which is shelf-stable. Simply reconstitute with water according to package directions for the amount indicated in the recipe. This is also a great solution for cooks who won't be able to use up fresh buttermilk within a reasonable amount of time.

buttermilk pie

shoo fly pie

1 cup all-purpose flour
$2/3$ cup packed brown sugar
$1/4$ cup ($1/2$ stick) plus 1 tablespoon unsalted butter, cubed, divided
3 eggs, beaten
$1/2$ cup molasses
$1/2$ teaspoon baking soda
$2/3$ cup hot water
1 unbaked deep-dish 9-inch pie crust
Whipped cream (optional)

1. Preheat oven to 325°F. Combine flour and brown sugar in medium bowl.

2. For topping, transfer $1/2$ cup flour mixture to small bowl. Cut in 1 tablespoon butter with pastry blender or two knives until mixture resembles coarse crumbs.

3. Melt remaining $1/4$ cup butter; cool slightly. Combine eggs, molasses and melted butter in large bowl. Gradually stir in flour mixture until well blended. Stir in baking soda. Gradually stir in water until blended. Pour into crust. Sprinkle with topping.

4. Bake 40 minutes or until filling is puffy and set. Cool completely on wire rack. Serve with whipped cream, if desired.   *Makes 8 servings*

shoo fly pie

lime chiffon pie

²/₃ cup boiling water
1 package (4-serving size) JELL-O® Lime Flavor Sugar Free
    Low Calorie Gelatin
Ice cubes
½ cup cold water
1½ teaspoons grated lime peel
2 tablespoons lime juice
2 cups thawed COOL WHIP FREE® Whipped Topping
1 ready-to-use reduced-fat graham cracker crumb crust (6 ounces)

STIR boiling water into dry gelatin mix in large bowl at least 2 minutes or until completely dissolved. Add enough ice to cold water to measure 1 cup. Add to gelatin; stir until ice is completely melted. Stir in lime peel and juice.

ADD whipped topping; stir with wire whisk until well blended. Refrigerate 15 to 20 minutes or until mixture is very thick and will mound. Spoon into crust.

REFRIGERATE at least 4 hours or overnight. Store leftover pie in refrigerator.
Makes 8 servings

For a variation of this refreshing dessert, prepare as directed using JELL-O® Brand Lemon Flavor Sugar Free Low Calorie Gelatin, lemon peel and lemon juice.

lime chiffon pie

classic apple pie

1 package (about 15 ounces) refrigerated pie crusts
6 cups sliced peeled Granny Smith, Crispin or other firm-fleshed
    apples (about 6 medium)
$\frac{1}{2}$ cup sugar
1 tablespoon cornstarch
2 teaspoons lemon juice
$\frac{1}{2}$ teaspoon ground cinnamon
$\frac{1}{2}$ teaspoon vanilla
$\frac{1}{8}$ teaspoon salt
$\frac{1}{8}$ teaspoon ground nutmeg
$\frac{1}{8}$ teaspoon ground cloves
1 tablespoon whipping cream

1. Let crusts stand at room temperature 15 minutes. Preheat oven to 350°F. Line 9-inch pie plate with one crust.

2. Combine apples, sugar, cornstarch, lemon juice, cinnamon, vanilla, salt, nutmeg and cloves in large bowl. Pour into crust. Place second crust over apples; crimp edge to seal.

3. Cut four slits in top crust; brush with cream. Bake 40 minutes or until crust is golden brown. Cool completely on wire rack.   *Makes 8 servings*

classic apple pie

mini libby's® famous pumpkin pies

¾ cup sugar
1 teaspoon ground cinnamon
½ teaspoon salt
½ teaspoon ground ginger
¼ teaspoon ground cloves
2 eggs
1 can (15 ounces) LIBBY'S® 100% Pure Pumpkin
1 can (12 fluid ounces) NESTLÉ® CARNATION® Evaporated Milk
4 (1-cup volume *each*) 4-inch mini pie shells

PREHEAT oven to 425°F.

MIX sugar, cinnamon, salt, ginger and cloves in small bowl. Beat eggs lightly in large bowl. Stir in pumpkin and sugar-spice mixture. Gradually stir in evaporated milk.

POUR into shells.

BAKE for 15 minutes. Reduce oven temperature to 350°F.; bake for 30 to 35 minutes or until knife inserted near center comes out clean. Cool on wire rack for 2 hours. Serve immediately or refrigerate. (Do not freeze as this may cause filling to separate from the crust.)   *Makes 4 mini pies*

Note: You may use one refrigerated or homemade single-crust pie pastry to make four mini pie shells. Lay rim of mini pie pan on rolled-out dough. Cut circle ½-inch larger than pan to allow for dough to form fluted edge.

Prep Time: 8 minutes | Cook Time: 45 minutes | Cool Time: 2 hours

mini libby's® famous pumpkin pies

lemon chess pie

  ½ (about 15-ounce) package refrigerated pie crusts
  3 eggs
  2 egg yolks
1¾ cups sugar
  ½ cup half-and-half
  ⅓ cup lemon juice
  ¼ cup melted butter
  3 tablespoons grated lemon peel
  2 tablespoons all-purpose flour
    Whipped cream (optional)

1. Let crust stand at room temperature 15 minutes. Preheat oven to 325°F. Line 9-inch pie plate with crust; flute edge.

2. Whisk eggs and egg yolks in large bowl. Whisk in sugar, half-and-half, lemon juice, butter, lemon peel and flour until well blended. Pour into crust.

3. Bake 40 minutes or until almost set. Cool completely on wire rack. Refrigerate 2 hours or until ready to serve. Serve with whipped cream, if desired.   *Makes 8 servings*

Note: To determine doneness, carefully shake pie. It is done when only the center 2 inches jiggle.

blueberry pie

Cream Cheese Pastry (recipe follows)
2 pints (4 cups) fresh or thawed frozen blueberries
2 tablespoons cornstarch
$2/3$ cup no-sugar-added blueberry preserves, melted
$1/4$ teaspoon ground nutmeg
1 egg yolk
1 tablespoon sour cream

1. Preheat oven to 425°F. Roll out one disc pastry into 11-inch circle on floured surface. Line 9-inch pie plate with pastry.

2. Combine blueberries and cornstarch in medium bowl; toss lightly to coat. Add preserves and nutmeg; mix lightly. Spoon into crust.

3. Roll out remaining disc pastry into 11-inch circle; place over fruit mixture. Turn edge under; flute. Cut several slits or circle in top crust. If desired, cut leaves from pastry scraps to decorate top of pie. Bake 10 minutes.

4. Reduce oven temperature to 350°F. Combine egg yolk and sour cream in small bowl; brush lightly over crust. Bake 40 minutes or until crust is golden brown. Cool 15 minutes on wire rack. Serve warm, at room temperature or chilled. *Makes 8 servings*

cream cheese pastry

$1\frac{1}{4}$ cups all-purpose flour
$1/2$ cup butter or shortening
3 ounces cream cheese, cubed
1 teaspoon vanilla

1. Place flour in large bowl. Cut in butter with pastry blender or two knives until mixture resembles coarse crumbs. Cut in cream cheese and vanilla until mixture forms dough.

2. Divide dough in half. Form each half into disc; wrap in plastic wrap. Refrigerate 30 minutes. *Makes pastry for one 9-inch pie*

blueberry pie

deep-dish peach custard pie

3½ cups (about 7 medium) peeled, pitted and sliced peaches
1 *unbaked* 9-inch (4-cup volume) deep-dish pie shell
1 can (14 ounces) NESTLÉ® CARNATION® Sweetened Condensed Milk
2 large eggs
¼ cup butter or margarine, melted
1 to 3 teaspoons lemon juice
½ teaspoon ground cinnamon
Dash ground nutmeg
Streusel Topping (recipe follows)

PREHEAT oven to 425°F.

ARRANGE peaches in pie shell. Combine sweetened condensed milk, eggs, butter, lemon juice, cinnamon and nutmeg in large mixer bowl; beat until smooth. Pour over peaches.

BAKE for 10 minutes. Sprinkle with Streusel Topping. Reduce oven temperature to 350°F.; bake for an additional 55 to 60 minutes or until knife inserted near center comes out clean. Cool on wire rack.

Makes 8 servings

Streusel Topping: Combine ⅓ cup all-purpose flour, ⅓ cup packed brown sugar and ⅓ cup chopped walnuts in medium bowl. Cut in 2 tablespoons butter or margarine with pastry blender or two knives until mixture resembles coarse crumbs.

deep-dish peach custard pie

enlightened fresh triple-berry pie

½ (about 15-ounce) package refrigerated pie crusts
1 lemon
4 cups strawberries, quartered, divided
½ cup sugar
½ cup water
2 tablespoons cornstarch
1 cup blueberries
1 cup raspberries
½ teaspoon vanilla or almond extract

1. Let crust stand at room temperature 15 minutes. Preheat oven to 475°F. Line deep-dish 9-inch pie pan with crust; flute edge. Prick holes in bottom and side with fork. Bake 12 minutes or until light brown. Place on wire rack. Finely grate lemon peel over crust; cool completely.

2. Combine 1 cup strawberries, sugar, water and cornstarch in blender; blend until smooth. Transfer to large saucepan. Bring to a boil over medium-high heat. Boil 1 minute, stirring constantly. Remove from heat. Let stand 10 to 15 minutes.

3. Add remaining strawberries, blueberries, raspberries and vanilla to strawberry mixture; stir gently. Spoon into crust. Cover with plastic wrap. Refrigerate until firm.

Makes 8 servings

enlightened fresh triple-berry pie

raspberry buttermilk pie

1 unbaked deep-dish 9-inch pie crust
3 eggs
2 tablespoons all-purpose flour
1 cup buttermilk
¾ cup plus 2 tablespoons sugar
¼ cup (½ stick) unsalted butter, melted
¼ cup honey
¼ teaspoon salt
½ teaspoon vanilla
1½ cups raspberries (see Tip)

1. Preheat oven to 425°F. Place crust on rimmed baking sheet. Bake 5 minutes. (It is not necessary to weigh down crust.) Remove from oven; press down any areas that puff up.

2. *Reduce oven temperature to 350°F.* Beat eggs and flour in large bowl until blended. Beat in buttermilk, sugar, butter, honey, salt and vanilla until sugar is dissolved. Gently stir in raspberries. Pour into crust.

3. Bake 30 minutes. If crust browns too quickly, tent pie with foil. Bake 20 minutes or until knife inserted near center comes out clean. Let stand 30 minutes before slicing.   *Makes 6 servings*

TIP Do not substitute frozen fruit for this recipe. While freezing can preserve fruits at the height of ripeness, it can also lead to textural changes when thawed. Raspberries are particularly fragile. Freezing and thawing these delicate berries can result in a mushy texture and a watery consistency that will cause the color to bleed into the surrounding buttermilk custard.

raspberry buttermilk pie

apple & cherry pie

2 cups all-purpose flour
$\frac{1}{2}$ cup plus 2$\frac{1}{2}$ tablespoons sugar, divided
$\frac{1}{2}$ teaspoon salt
3 tablespoons *each* butter and shortening
1 tablespoon cider vinegar
5 to 6 tablespoons water
$\frac{1}{2}$ cup dried cherries
$\frac{1}{4}$ cup apple juice
1 tablespoon cornstarch
2$\frac{1}{4}$ teaspoons ground cinnamon, divided
6 cups sliced peeled Jonagold or Golden Delicious apples
1 teaspoon vanilla
1 egg white, beaten

1. Combine flour, 2 tablespoons sugar and salt in medium bowl. Cut in butter and shortening with pastry blender or two knives until mixture resembles coarse crumbs. Add vinegar and 4 tablespoons water, stirring with fork. Add additional water, 1 tablespoon at a time, until dough forms. Divide dough into thirds. Shape one piece into disc; wrap in plastic wrap. Combine remaining 2 pieces dough, forming larger disc; wrap in plastic wrap. Refrigerate 30 minutes.

2. Preheat oven to 375°F. Combine cherries and apple juice in small microwavable bowl; microwave on HIGH 1$\frac{1}{2}$ minutes. Let stand 15 minutes. Combine $\frac{1}{2}$ cup sugar, cornstarch and 2 teaspoons cinnamon in large bowl. Add apples and vanilla; toss to combine.

3. Coat 9-inch pie plate with nonstick cooking spray. Roll larger disc of dough into 12-inch circle on floured surface. Line prepared pie plate. Spoon apple mixture into crust. Roll smaller disc of dough into 10-inch circle. Cut into $\frac{1}{2}$-inch strips. Arrange in lattice design over fruit. Seal and flute edge; brush with egg white.

4. Combine remaining $\frac{1}{2}$ tablespoon sugar and $\frac{1}{4}$ teaspoon cinnamon; sprinkle over pie. Bake 45 minutes or until apples are tender and crust is golden brown. Cool 30 minutes on wire rack. Serve warm or at room temperature.

Makes 8 servings

apple & cherry pie

citrus sorbet pie

⅔ cup boiling water
1 package (4-serving size) JELL-O® Orange Flavor Gelatin
1 cup orange sherbet
2 cups thawed COOL WHIP® Whipped Topping
2 cups JET-PUFFED® Miniature Marshmallows
1 can (8 ounces) crushed pineapple, drained
1 HONEY MAID® Graham Pie Crust (6 ounces)

STIR boiling water into dry gelatin mix in large bowl at least 2 minutes or until completely dissolved. Add sherbet; stir until sherbet is completely melted and mixture is slightly thickened. Add whipped topping, marshmallows and pineapple; stir gently with wire whisk until well blended. Refrigerate 10 minutes or until mixture is very thick and will mound.

POUR into crust.

FREEZE 4 hours or until firm. Store leftover pie in freezer.

Makes 8 servings

Variation: Prepare as directed, using JELL-O® Lime Flavor Gelatin and lemon sherbet.

Prep Time: 10 minutes | Total Time: 4 hours 20 minutes (includes freezing)

citrus sorbet pie

spiced peach pie

Double-Crust Pie Pastry (recipe follows)
1 egg, separated
2 tablespoons cornstarch
2 teaspoons ground cinnamon
1/2 teaspoon ground nutmeg
1/8 teaspoon salt
1/2 cup unsweetened apple juice concentrate
1 teaspoon vanilla
5 cups sliced peeled peaches
1 tablespoon butter
1 teaspoon cold water

1. Preheat oven to 400°F. Roll out one disc pastry into 11-inch circle. Line 9-inch pie plate with pastry. Beat egg white until frothy; brush over pastry.

2. Combine cornstarch, cinnamon, nutmeg and salt in large bowl. Stir in juice concentrate and vanilla. Add peaches; toss lightly to coat. Spoon into crust; dot with butter.

3. Roll out remaining disc pastry into 10-inch circle. Cut into 1/2-inch-wide strips. Arrange in lattice design over peaches. Seal and flute edge. Whisk egg yolk and water in small bowl; brush over pastry.

4. Bake 50 minutes or until crust is golden brown and filling is thick and bubbly.* Cool on wire rack. Serve warm, at room temperature or chilled.

Makes 8 servings

Pie may be covered loosely with foil after 30 minutes of baking to prevent overbrowning, if desired.

Double-Crust Pie Pastry: Combine 2 1/2 cups all-purpose flour, 1 teaspoon salt and 1 teaspoon sugar in large bowl. Cut in 1 cup (2 sticks) cubed unsalted butter with pastry blender or two knives until mixture resembles coarse crumbs. Drizzle 1/3 cup water over flour mixture, 2 tablespoons at a time, stirring just until dough comes together. Divide dough in half. Form each half into disc; wrap in plastic wrap. Refrigerate 30 minutes.

spiced peach pie

cranberry apple nut pie

Rich Pie Pastry (recipe follows)
1 cup sugar
3 tablespoons all-purpose flour
¼ teaspoon salt
4 cups sliced peeled tart apples
2 cups fresh cranberries
½ cup golden raisins
½ cup coarsely chopped pecans
1 tablespoon grated lemon peel
2 tablespoons butter, cubed
1 egg, beaten

1. Preheat oven to 425°F. Roll out one disc pastry into 11-inch circle on floured surface. Line 9-inch pie plate with pastry.

2. Combine sugar, flour and salt in large bowl. Stir in apples, cranberries, raisins, pecans and lemon peel; toss well. Transfer to crust; dot with butter.

3. Roll out remaining disc pastry into 11-inch circle. Place over filling. Trim and seal edge; flute. Reroll scraps and cut into decorative shapes. Moisten pastry cutouts with water and adhere to top crust as desired. Cut three slits in center of top crust. Lightly brush top crust with egg.

4. Bake 35 minutes or until apples are tender and crust is golden brown. Cool 15 minutes on wire rack. Serve warm or cool completely.

Makes 8 servings

Rich Pie Pastry: Combine 2 cups all-purpose flour and ¼ teaspoon salt in medium bowl. Cut in 6 tablespoons cubed unsalted butter and 6 tablespoons shortening with pastry blender or two knives until mixture resembles coarse crumbs. Sprinkle 6 tablespoons water, 1 tablespoon at a time, over flour mixture, mixing until dough forms. Divide dough in half. Form each half into disc; wrap in plastic wrap. Refrigerate 30 minutes.

cranberry apple nut pie

so-easy peach pie

½ (about 15-ounce) package refrigerated pie crusts
1 package (16 ounces) frozen peaches, thawed, juice reserved
2 teaspoons cornstarch
½ cup golden raisins
4 tablespoons sugar, divided
1 teaspoon vanilla
¼ teaspoon ground cinnamon (optional)

1. Let crust stand at room temperature 15 minutes. Preheat oven to 450°F. Coat large nonstick baking sheet with nonstick cooking spray.

2. Unroll crust on prepared baking sheet. Roll or flute edge, if desired. Prick holes in crust with fork. Bake 10 minutes or until golden brown.

3. Combine peach juice and cornstarch in large nonstick skillet until cornstarch is dissolved. Add peaches and raisins. Bring to a boil over high heat; boil 2 minutes, stirring occasionally. Remove from heat; add 3 tablespoons sugar, vanilla and cinnamon, if desired.

4. Slide baked crust over peach mixture in skillet. Sprinkle with remaining 1 tablespoon sugar.   *Makes 8 servings*

Variation: Substitute 1 teaspoon almond extract for the vanilla.

so-easy peach pie

blackberry custard pie

Single-Crust Pie Pastry (recipe follows)
$\frac{1}{2}$ cup sugar
3 tablespoons cornstarch
$1\frac{1}{4}$ cups milk
1 tablespoon lemon juice
2 teaspoons grated lemon peel
2 eggs, lightly beaten
1 pint blackberries

1. Preheat oven to 425°F. Roll out pastry into 11-inch circle on floured surface. Line 9-inch pie plate with pastry; flute edge. Cut square of foil about 4 inches larger than pie plate. Line crust with foil; fill with dried beans, uncooked rice or ceramic pie weights. Bake 10 minutes or until set.

2. Remove foil lining and beans. Bake crust 5 minutes or until lightly browned. Cool completely on wire rack.

3. Combine sugar and cornstarch in small saucepan. Stir in milk, lemon juice and lemon peel; cook and stir over medium heat until mixture boils and thickens. Boil 1 minute, stirring constantly. Stir about $\frac{1}{2}$ cup hot milk mixture into eggs; stir egg mixture back into saucepan. Cook over low heat until thickened, stirring constantly. Spoon into crust. Cool to room temperature; refrigerate 3 hours or until set. Arrange blackberries on custard. *Makes 8 servings*

Single-Crust Pie Pastry: Combine $1\frac{1}{4}$ cups all-purpose flour and $\frac{1}{2}$ teaspoon salt in medium bowl. Cut in 3 tablespoons shortening and 3 tablespoons cubed unsalted butter with pastry blender or two knives until mixture resembles coarse crumbs. Combine 3 tablespoons water and $\frac{1}{2}$ teaspoon cider vinegar in small bowl. Add to flour mixture; mix with fork until dough forms, adding additional water as needed. Form dough into disc; wrap in plastic wrap. Refrigerate 30 minutes.

blackberry custard pie

strawberry rhubarb pie

Double-Crust Pie Pastry (recipe follows)
1 1/2 cups sugar
1/2 cup cornstarch
2 tablespoons quick-cooking tapioca
1 tablespoon grated lemon peel
1/4 teaspoon ground allspice
4 cups sliced (1-inch pieces) rhubarb
3 cups sliced strawberries
1 egg, lightly beaten

1. Preheat oven to 425°F. Roll out one disc pastry into 11-inch circle on floured surface. Line 9-inch pie plate with pastry.

2. Combine sugar, cornstarch, tapioca, lemon peel and allspice in large bowl. Add rhubarb and strawberries; toss to coat. Transfer to crust.

3. Roll out remaining disc pastry into 10-inch circle. Cut into 1/2-inch-wide strips. Arrange in lattice design over fruit. Seal and flute edge. Brush pastry with egg.

4. Bake 50 minutes or until filling is thick and bubbly. Cool on wire rack. Serve warm or at room temperature.   *Makes 8 servings*

Double-Crust Pie Pastry: Combine 2 1/2 cups all-purpose flour, 1 teaspoon salt and 1 teaspoon sugar in large bowl. Cut in 1 cup (2 sticks) cubed unsalted butter with pastry blender or two knives until mixture resembles coarse crumbs. Drizzle 1/3 cup water over flour mixture, 2 tablespoons at a time, stirring just until dough comes together. Divide dough in half. Form each half into disc; wrap in plastic wrap. Refrigerate 30 minutes.

strawberry rhubarb pie

celia's flat fruit pie

2 packages (8 ounces each) dried mixed fruit
3 cups water
$\frac{1}{2}$ cup sugar
$\frac{1}{2}$ teaspoon ground cinnamon
$\frac{1}{4}$ teaspoon ground cloves
1 teaspoon lemon juice
Flaky Pastry (recipe follows)

1. Combine fruit, water, sugar, cinnamon and cloves in 3-quart saucepan. Cook over medium heat until sugar is dissolved, stirring occasionally. Reduce heat to low; cover and simmer 45 minutes or until fruit is tender. Transfer to blender or food processor; process until fruit is coarsely puréed. (Purée should measure 3 cups. If purée measures more, return to saucepan and cook, stirring frequently, to reduce to 3 cups.) Stir in lemon juice. Cool completely.

2. Preheat oven to 400°F. Roll one disc pastry into 13-inch circle on floured surface. Place on 12-inch pizza pan, trimming to leave $\frac{1}{2}$-inch overhang. Spread fruit purée over pastry. Roll out remaining disc pastry into 13-inch circle; place over filling. Cut slits or design in center. Fold edge of top crust under edge of bottom crust; flute. Bake 35 minutes or until golden brown. Cool 1 hour on wire rack. *Makes 12 servings*

Flaky Pastry: Combine $3\frac{1}{3}$ cups all-purpose flour and $\frac{3}{4}$ teaspoon salt in medium bowl. Cut in 1 cup shortening with pastry blender or two knives until mixture resembles coarse crumbs. Sprinkle 6 tablespoons water, 1 tablespoon at a time, over flour mixture, mixing until dough forms. Divide dough in half. Form each half into disc; wrap in plastic wrap. Refrigerate 30 minutes.

celia's flat fruit pie

apple-pear praline pie

6 cups sliced peeled Granny Smith apples
3 cups sliced peeled pears
¾ cup granulated sugar
¼ cup plus 1 tablespoon all-purpose flour, divided
4 teaspoons ground cinnamon
¼ teaspoon salt
   Double-Crust Pie Pastry (recipe follows)
½ cup plus 2 tablespoons butter, divided
1 cup packed brown sugar
¼ cup half-and-half
1 cup chopped pecans

1. Preheat oven to 350°F. Combine apples, pears, granulated sugar, ¼ cup flour, cinnamon and salt in large bowl; toss gently. Let stand 15 minutes.

2. Roll out one disc pastry into 11-inch circle on floured surface. Line deep-dish 9-inch pie pan with pastry; sprinkle with remaining 1 tablespoon flour. Spoon apple and pear mixture into crust; dot with 2 tablespoons butter.

3. Roll out remaining disc pastry into 10-inch circle. Place over fruit; flute edge. Cut slits in top crust. Bake 50 minutes.

4. Melt remaining ½ cup butter in small saucepan over low heat. Stir in brown sugar and half-and-half. Bring to a boil, stirring constantly. Remove from heat; stir in pecans. Spread over top of pie.

5. Place pie on baking sheet; bake 5 minutes. Cool 15 minutes on wire rack. Serve warm or at room temperature.   *Makes 8 servings*

Double-Crust Pie Pastry: Combine 2½ cups all-purpose flour, 1 teaspoon salt and 1 teaspoon sugar in large bowl. Cut in 1 cup (2 sticks) cubed unsalted butter with pastry blender or two knives until mixture resembles coarse crumbs. Drizzle ⅓ cup water over flour mixture, 2 tablespoons at a time, stirring just until dough comes together. Divide dough in half. Form each half into disc; wrap in plastic wrap. Refrigerate 30 minutes.

apple-pear praline pie

summer berry pie

 ¾ cup sugar
 3 tablespoons cornstarch
1½ cups water
 1 package (4-serving size) JELL-O® Strawberry Flavor Gelatin
 1 cup *each* blueberries, raspberries and sliced strawberries
 1 HONEY MAID® Graham Pie Crust (6 ounces)
1½ cups thawed COOL WHIP® Whipped Topping

MIX sugar and cornstarch in medium saucepan. Gradually add water, stirring until well blended. Bring to boil over medium heat, stirring constantly; boil 1 minute. Remove from heat. Add dry gelatin mix; stir until dissolved. Stir in fruit.

POUR into crust.

REFRIGERATE 3 hours or until firm. Top with whipped topping just before serving. Store any leftover pie in refrigerator.   *Makes 10 servings*

summer berry pie

strawberry cool 'n' easy pie

> 1 package (4-serving size) JELL-O® Strawberry Flavor Gelatin
> $2/3$ cup boiling water
> $1/2$ cup cold water
>   Ice cubes
> 1 tub (8 ounces) COOL WHIP® Whipped Topping, thawed
> 1 cup chopped strawberries
> 1 prepared graham cracker crumb crust (6 ounces)

DISSOLVE gelatin completely in boiling water in large bowl. Mix cold water and ice to make 1 cup. Add to gelatin, stirring until slightly thickened. Remove any remaining ice.

STIR in whipped topping with wire whisk until smooth. Mix in strawberries. Refrigerate 20 to 30 minutes or until mixture is very thick and will mound. Spoon into crust.

REFRIGERATE 4 hours or until firm. Garnish with additional whipped topping and strawberries. Store leftover pie in refrigerator.

Makes 8 servings

chocolate velvet pie

    1 unbaked deep-dish 9-inch pie crust
  ¾ cup half-and-half
    4 ounces semisweet chocolate
    3 eggs
    1 egg yolk
  10 tablespoons sugar, divided
    1 teaspoon vanilla, divided
  ⅛ teaspoon salt
    1 package (8 ounces) cream cheese, softened
  ¼ cup whipping cream
      Raspberries and semisweet chocolate curls (optional)

1. Preheat oven to 400°F. Prick holes in bottom of crust with fork. Bake 10 minutes or until light brown. Cool completely on wire rack.

2. *Reduce oven temperature to 350°F.* Combine half-and-half and chocolate in medium heavy saucepan over medium-low heat; cook and stir until chocolate is melted. Remove from heat.

3. Beat 2 eggs and egg yolk in small bowl with electric mixer at low speed until blended. Beat into chocolate mixture. Beat in 6 tablespoons sugar, ½ teaspoon vanilla and salt until well blended. Spread evenly in crust.

4. Beat cream cheese and remaining 4 tablespoons sugar in medium bowl at medium-high speed until smooth. Beat in whipping cream, remaining egg and ½ teaspoon vanilla until well blended. Gently drop cream cheese mixture by spoonfuls over filling to cover surface of pie.

5. Bake 40 minutes or until set. Cool completely on wire rack. Cover and refrigerate 2 hours before serving. Garnish with raspberries and chocolate curls. *Makes 10 servings*

chocolate velvet pie

frozen margarita pie

CRUST
  10 ORTEGA® Yellow Corn Taco Shells
  $\frac{1}{2}$ cup (1 stick) butter
  $\frac{1}{2}$ cup granulated sugar

FILLING
  1 can (14 ounces) sweetened condensed milk
  $\frac{1}{3}$ cup frozen limeade, thawed
  2 tablespoons orange juice
  1 drop green food coloring
  1 cup whipping cream
  Lime curls (optional)

PLACE taco shells in food processor and pulse until evenly ground.

MELT butter in medium saucepan over low heat. Remove from heat. Stir in taco crumbs and sugar until well blended. Press firmly over bottom and up sides of 9-inch pie plate. Place in freezer until firm.

COMBINE sweetened condensed milk, limeade, orange juice and food coloring in large mixing bowl.

WHIP cream until soft peaks form. Fold whipped cream gently into condensed milk mixture until blended. Pour into prepared crust.

FREEZE, uncovered, 4 hours or until firm. Let stand 10 minutes before serving. Garnish with lime curls, if desired.   *Makes 8 servings*

 To crush taco shells without a food processor, place them in a resealable food storage bag and run a rolling pin over the shells until they're evenly crushed.

frozen margarita pie

chocolate mint cookie pie

30 marshmallows
$\frac{1}{2}$ cup milk
4 ounces bittersweet chocolate, finely chopped
2 ounces unsweetened chocolate, finely chopped
$\frac{1}{2}$ teaspoon mint extract
1$\frac{1}{2}$ cups whipping cream
1 (6-ounce) chocolate crumb pie crust
1 container (8 ounces) whipped topping
12 chocolate mint sandwich cookies, chopped

1. Combine marshmallows and milk in medium saucepan; cook over medium heat 7 minutes or until melted and smooth, stirring constantly. Remove from heat. Stir in chocolate and mint extract until melted and smooth.

2. Beat cream in medium bowl with electric mixer at medium speed until stiff peaks form. Fold one fourth of whipped cream into chocolate mixture just until lightened. Fold chocolate mixture into remaining whipped cream until blended. Spread evenly in crust.

3. Spread whipping topping over top. Sprinkle with cookie pieces. Refrigerate 3 hours or overnight.   *Makes 8 to 10 servings*

chocolate mint cookie pie

pumpkin ice cream pie with caramel sauce

25 gingersnap cookies, finely crushed
¼ cup (½ stick) unsalted butter, melted
2 tablespoons granulated sugar
1 quart pumpkin ice cream, softened
1 cup packed dark brown sugar
½ cup whipping cream
6 tablespoons (¾ stick) unsalted butter, cubed
¼ cup light corn syrup
½ teaspoon salt
1 cup chopped pecans, toasted*

To toast pecans, spread them on a baking sheet and place in a preheated 350°F oven for 6 to 8 minutes.

1. Preheat oven to 350°F. Coat 9-inch pie plate with nonstick cooking spray.

2. Combine cookie crumbs, melted butter and granulated sugar in medium bowl. Press onto bottom and up side of prepared pie plate. Bake 8 minutes. Cool completely on wire rack.

3. Spread ice cream evenly in crust. Cover and freeze 1 hour.

4. Whisk brown sugar, cream, cubed butter, corn syrup and salt in medium saucepan over medium-high heat until sugar is dissolved. Boil 1 minute without stirring. Cool completely. Drizzle over pie. Sprinkle with pecans.

Makes 8 servings

pumpkin ice cream pie with caramel sauce

chilly lemon pie

1¼ cups graham cracker crumbs (about 1 package)
¼ cup (½ stick) butter, melted
1 tablespoon sugar
1 tablespoon plus 1 teaspoon grated lemon peel, divided
1 can (14 ounces) sweetened condensed milk
½ cup lemon juice (about 3 lemons)
　Lemon slices and raspberries (optional)

1. Preheat oven to 350°F. Combine graham cracker crumbs, butter, sugar and 1 teaspoon lemon peel in 9-inch pie plate. Press onto bottom and up side of pie plate. Bake 7 to 10 minutes or until golden brown. Cool completely on wire rack.

2. Whisk sweetened condensed milk, lemon juice and remaining 1 tablespoon lemon peel in medium bowl. Pour into crust.

3. Cover and refrigerate 3 hours or until set. Garnish with lemon slices and raspberries. Refrigerate any leftovers.　　　　*Makes 8 servings*

TIP This simple recipe lends itself freely to variation. You can experiment with any kind of citrus. Simply replace the lemon juice and grated lemon peel with the same amount of lime, orange or grapefruit.

chilly lemon pie

triple-layer mud pie

3 squares BAKER'S® Semi-Sweet Baking Chocolate, melted
¼ cup canned sweetened condensed milk
1 OREO® Pie Crust (6 ounces)
¾ cup chopped PLANTER'S® Pecans, toasted
2 cups cold milk
2 packages (4-serving size each) JELL-O® Chocolate Flavor Instant
    Pudding & Pie Filling
1 tub (8 ounces) COOL WHIP® Whipped Topping, thawed, divided

MIX chocolate and condensed milk until well blended. Pour into crust.
Sprinkle with pecans.

POUR milk into large bowl. Add dry pudding mixes. Beat with wire whisk
2 minutes or until well blended. (Mixture will be thick.) Spoon 1½ cups
of the pudding over pecans in crust. Add half of the whipped topping to
remaining pudding. Stir with wire whisk until well blended. Spread over
pudding layer in crust; top with remaining whipped topping.

STIR Spread over pudding in crust. Top with remaining whipped topping.

REFRIGERATE 3 hours. Store leftover pie in refrigerator.

Makes 10 servings

Prep Time: 15 minutes | Chill Time: 3 hours

triple-layer mud pie

key lime cheesecake pie

1¼ cups finely crushed coconut bar cookies
¼ cup (½ stick) butter or margarine, melted
3 tablespoons sugar
2 packages (8 ounces each) PHILADELPHIA® Cream Cheese, softened
1 can (14 ounces) sweetened condensed milk
½ teaspoons grated lime peel
½ cup lime juice
    Few drops green food coloring (optional)

HEAT oven to 350°F. Mix crumbs, butter and sugar; press firmly onto bottom and up side of 9-inch pie plate. Bake 10 minutes. Cool.

BEAT cream cheese and sweetened condensed milk in large bowl with electric mixer on medium speed until well blended. Add peel, juice and food coloring; mix well. Pour into crust.

REFRIGERATE at least 8 hours or overnight. Store leftover pie in refrigerator. *Makes 10 servings*

Special Extra: Garnish with lime slices and fresh mint just before serving.

TIP To soften, place unwrapped package of cream cheese in microwaveable bowl. Microwave on HIGH 15 seconds or just until softened. Add 15 seconds for each additional package of cream cheese.

key lime cheesecake pie

granny's no-crust chocolate pie

$\frac{1}{2}$ cup granulated sugar
3 tablespoons all-purpose flour
3 tablespoons cocoa powder
$\frac{1}{8}$ teaspoon salt
2 cups milk
3 eggs, separated
2 tablespoons butter
1 teaspoon vanilla
3 tablespoons superfine sugar

1. Grease 9-inch pie pan. Combine granulated sugar, flour, cocoa and salt in medium saucepan. Gradually whisk in milk and egg yolks; cook and stir over low heat until smooth and thickened. Remove from heat; stir in butter and vanilla. Pour into prepared pie pan; refrigerate 1 hour or until set.

2. Preheat oven to 400°F. Whip egg whites in medium bowl with electric mixer at high speed until foamy. Add superfine sugar; beat until stiff peaks form. Top pie with meringue.

3. Bake 8 to 10 minutes or until meringue is golden brown. Cool 15 minutes on wire rack. *Makes 8 servings*

TIP Superfine sugar is finely granulated so that it dissolves readily. If you can't find it at the grocery store, you can create a reasonable substitute at home by processing regular granulated sugar in a food processor until it is very fine.

granny's no-crust chocolate pie

black bottom banana cream pie

25 NILLA® Wafers, finely crushed (about 1¼ cups crumbs)
6 tablespoons butter or margarine, melted, divided
2 tablespoons sugar
4 squares BAKER'S® Semi-Sweet Baking chocolate
2 large bananas, sliced
1 package (4-serving size) JELL-O® Vanilla Flavor Instant
    Pudding & Pie Filling
1¾ cups cold milk
1 cup thawed COOL WHIP® Whipped Topping

MIX crumbs, ¼ cup (4 tablespoons) of the melted butter and sugar in medium bowl. Remove 2 tablespoons of the crumb mixture; set aside for later use. Press remaining crumb mixture firmly onto bottom and up side of 9-inch pie plate; set aside.

MICROWAVE chocolate and remaining 2 tablespoons butter in medium microwaveable bowl on HIGH 1 minute or until butter is melted; stir until chocolate is completely melted. Spread evenly onto bottom of crust; top with bananas. Set aside.

PREPARE pudding mix with the 1¾ cups milk as directed on package for pie; pour evenly over bananas. Refrigerate at least 4 hours or overnight. Top with whipped topping just before serving; sprinkle with reserved 2 tablespoons crumb mixture. Store leftover pie in refrigerator.

Makes 8 servings

Prep Time: 30 minutes | Chill Time: 4 hours

black bottom banana cream pie

baked alaska apple butter pie

Single-Crust Pie Pastry (recipe follows)
2 cups apple butter
1 can (13 ounces) evaporated milk
3 egg yolks, beaten
¼ cup packed brown sugar
1 pint butter pecan ice cream, softened
Brown Sugar Meringue (recipe follows)

1. Preheat oven to 425°F. Roll out pastry into 11-inch circle on floured surface. Line 9-inch pie plate with pastry; flute edge.

2. Combine apple butter, evaporated milk, egg yolks and brown sugar in medium bowl. Pour into crust. Bake 15 minutes. *Reduce oven temperature to 350°F.* Bake 45 minutes or until knife inserted into center comes out clean. Cool completely on wire rack. Cover and refrigerate 1 hour or until ready to serve.

3. Cover inside of 8-inch pie plate with plastic wrap. Spread ice cream in prepared pie plate. Cover and freeze until firm.

4. Just before serving, preheat oven to 500°F. Prepare Brown Sugar Meringue. Unmold ice cream and invert onto chilled pie. Remove plastic wrap. Cover entire surface of pie with meringue. Bake 2 minutes or until golden brown. Serve immediately. *Makes 8 servings*

Single-Crust Pie Pastry: Combine 1¼ cups flour and ½ teaspoon salt in medium bowl. Cut in 3 tablespoons shortening and 3 tablespoons cubed unsalted butter with pastry blender or two knives until mixture resembles coarse crumbs. Combine 3 tablespoons water and ½ teaspoon cider vinegar in small bowl. Add to flour mixture; mix with fork until dough forms, adding additional water as needed. Form dough into disc; wrap in plastic wrap. Refrigerate 30 minutes.

brown sugar meringue

  3 egg whites
  ¼ teaspoon cream of tartar
  ½ teaspoon vanilla
  6 tablespoons packed brown sugar

Beat egg whites and cream of tartar in small bowl with electric mixer at high speed until foamy. Beat in vanilla. Add brown sugar, 1 tablespoon at a time, beating until stiff peaks form.

ginger cream banana pie

  1½ cups gingersnap cookie crumbs
  ¼ cup margarine, softened
  2¼ cups milk
  1 package (5.1 ounces) instant vanilla pudding (6 servings)
  1 tablespoon crystallized ginger
  1 tablespoon grated orange peel
  4 firm medium DOLE® Bananas

• Combine gingersnap crumbs and margarine in bowl. Press onto bottom and up side of 9-inch pie plate. Bake at 350°F 5 minutes. Cool.

• Combine milk, pudding, ginger and orange peel until well blended. Slice 2 bananas into bottom of pie shell. Cover with one-half filling. Slice remaining bananas over filling. Top with remaining filling. Press plastic wrap on surface. Refrigerate 3 hours. Garnish with additional banana slices, orange curls and edible flowers, if desired.   *Makes 8 servings*

Prep Time: 25 minutes | Chill Time: 3 hours

chocolate and vanilla-swirled cheese pie

2 packages (8 ounces each) cream cheese, softened
$\frac{1}{2}$ cup sugar
1 teaspoon vanilla extract
2 eggs
1 prepared deep-dish crumb crust (9 ounces)
1 cup HERSHEY'S SPECIAL DARK® Chocolate Chips
$\frac{1}{4}$ cup milk
Red raspberry jam (optional)

1. Heat oven to 350°F.

2. Beat cream cheese, sugar and vanilla in mixer bowl until well blended. Add eggs; mix thoroughly. Spread 2 cups batter in crumb crust.

3. Place chocolate chips in medium microwave-safe bowl. Microwave at MEDIUM (50%) 1 minute; stir. If necessary, microwave an additional 15 seconds at a time, stirring after each heating, until chocolate is melted and smooth when stirred. Cool slightly. Add melted chocolate and milk to remaining batter; blend thoroughly. Drop chocolate batter by tablespoonfuls onto vanilla batter. Gently swirl with knife for marbled effect.

4. Bake 30 to 35 minutes or until center is almost set. Cool; refrigerate several hours or overnight. Drizzle with warmed red raspberry jam, if desired. Cover and refrigerate leftover pie.   *Makes 8 servings*

chocolate and vanilla-swirled cheese pie

lemon-lime meringue pie

1 unbaked deep-dish 9-inch pie crust
4 eggs, separated
¾ cup plus 1 tablespoon sugar, divided
⅛ teaspoon salt
1 tablespoon cornstarch
½ cup whipping cream
3 tablespoons lemon juice
3 tablespoons lime juice
2 teaspoons grated lemon peel
2 teaspoons grated lime peel
2 tablespoons unsalted butter, cut in small pieces

1. Preheat oven to 400°F. Prick holes in bottom of crust with fork. Bake 10 minutes or until light brown. Cool completely on wire rack.

2. *Reduce oven temperature to 325°F.* Whisk egg yolks, ½ cup plus 1 tablespoon sugar and salt in medium saucepan. Stir cornstarch into cream in small bowl until smooth. Stir into egg yolk mixture.

3. Stir in lemon juice, lime juice, lemon peel and lime peel. Cook and stir over medium heat until thickened. Remove from heat; stir in butter until melted. Pour into crust.

4. Beat egg whites in medium bowl with electric mixer at medium speed until frothy. Add remaining ¼ cup sugar, 1 tablespoon at a time, beating at high speed after each addition until stiff peaks form. Gently spread meringue over filling.

5. Bake 20 minutes or until meringue is golden brown. Cool completely on wire rack. *Makes 8 servings*

lemon-lime meringue pie

confetti pie

1 cup boiling water
1 package (4-serving size) JELL-O® Brand Lemon Flavor Gelatin
½ cup cold water
1 cup boiling water
1 package (4-serving size) JELL-O® Brand Orange Flavor Gelatin
½ cup cold orange juice
2 cups thawed COOL WHIP® Whipped Topping
⅓ cup multi-colored sprinkles
1 HONEY MAID® Honey Graham Pie Crust (9 inch)

STIR 1 cup boiling water into lemon gelatin in medium bowl at least 2 minutes or until completely dissolved. Stir in cold water. Pour into 8-inch square pan. Refrigerate 4 hours or until firm. Cut into ½-inch cubes.

STIR 1 cup boiling water into orange gelatin in large bowl at least 2 minutes or until completely dissolved. Stir in orange juice. Refrigerate about 20 minutes or until slightly thickened (consistency of unbeaten egg whites). Gently stir in whipped topping. Gently stir in gelatin cubes and sprinkles. Refrigerate until mixture will mound. Pour into crust.

REFRIGERATE at least 4 hours or until firm. Garnish with additional whipped topping and sprinkles, if desired.   *Makes 8 servings*

Variation: Try Berry Blue or Lime Flavor Gelatin instead of Lemon Flavor when making the gelatin cubes.

confetti pie

peach cherry pie

½ (about 15-ounce) package refrigerated pie crusts
¾ cup granulated sugar
3 tablespoons quick-cooking tapioca
1 teaspoon grated lemon peel
½ teaspoon ground cinnamon
⅛ teaspoon salt
4 cups peach slices (about 7 medium)
2 cups Bing cherries, pitted
1 tablespoon lemon juice
2 tablespoons unsalted butter, cubed
    Brown Sugar Streusel Topping (recipe follows)
    Vanilla ice cream (optional)

1. Let crust stand at room temperature 15 minutes. Preheat oven to 375°F. Line 9-inch pie plate with crust; flute edge.

2. Combine granulated sugar, tapioca, lemon peel, cinnamon and salt in large bowl. Add peaches, cherries and lemon juice; toss until blended. Spread evenly in crust. Dot with butter.

3. Prepare Brown Sugar Streusel Topping; sprinkle over pie filling.

4. Bake 40 minutes or until bubbly. Cool 15 minutes on wire rack. Serve warm or at room temperature with ice cream, if desired. Refrigerate leftovers.
Makes 8 servings

Brown Sugar Streusel Topping: Combine ¾ cup old-fashioned oats, ⅓ cup all-purpose flour, ⅓ cup packed brown sugar and ¾ teaspoon ground cinnamon in medium bowl. Stir in 4 tablespoons melted unsalted butter until mixture resembles coarse crumbs.

chocolate & peanut pie

1½ cups all-purpose flour
½ cup plus 1 tablespoon sugar, divided
½ teaspoon salt, divided
½ cup (1 stick) unsalted butter, melted
¾ cup half-and-half
½ cup semisweet chocolate chips
3 eggs
½ teaspoon vanilla
½ cup caramel dessert topping
¾ cup honey-roasted peanuts

1. Preheat oven to 425°F. Combine flour, 1 tablespoon sugar and ¼ teaspoon salt in medium bowl. Slowly pour in melted butter, stirring until dough forms.

2. Transfer dough to 9-inch pie pan; press onto bottom and up side, forming high rim. Place on rimmed baking sheet. Bake 5 minutes. (It is not necessary to weigh down crust.)

3. *Reduce oven temperature to 350°F.* Combine half-and-half and chocolate chips in top of double boiler over simmering water. Cook until chocolate is melted, stirring occasionally. Remove from heat; stir in remaining ½ cup sugar and ¼ teaspoon salt. Beat in eggs, one at a time, until blended. Stir in vanilla.

4. Spread dessert topping evenly over bottom of crust; sprinkle with peanuts. Gently spoon chocolate mixture into crust. (Most peanuts will float to top.)

5. Bake 45 minutes or until set. Cool 15 minutes on wire rack. Refrigerate 4 hours or overnight. *Makes 8 servings*

chocolate & peanut pie

plum & walnut pie

Single-Crust Pie Pastry (recipe follows)
8 cups thinly sliced plums
$\frac{1}{3}$ cup granulated sugar
$\frac{1}{3}$ cup packed light brown sugar
3 to 4 tablespoons all-purpose flour
1 tablespoon honey
$\frac{1}{2}$ teaspoon ground cinnamon
$\frac{1}{4}$ teaspoon ground ginger
$\frac{1}{8}$ teaspoon salt
Oat Streusel (recipe follows)
$\frac{1}{2}$ cup candied walnuts

1. Preheat oven to 425°F. Roll out pastry into 11-inch circle on floured surface. Line 9-inch pie pan with pastry; flute edge.

2. Place plums in large bowl. Stir in granulated sugar, brown sugar, 3 tablespoons flour (use 4 tablespoons if plums are very juicy), honey, cinnamon, ginger and salt. Spread plum mixture evenly in crust. Prepare Oat Streusel; sprinkle over pie. Place pie on rimmed baking sheet.

3. Bake 15 minutes. *Reduce oven temperature to 350°F.* Sprinkle pie with walnuts. Bake 30 minutes. Lightly tent pie with foil. Bake 30 minutes or until filling is bubbly and crust is golden brown. Cool 30 minutes on wire rack.

Makes 8 servings

Single-Crust Pie Pastry: Combine $1\frac{1}{4}$ cups all-purpose flour and $\frac{1}{2}$ teaspoon salt in medium bowl. Cut in 3 tablespoons shortening and 3 tablespoons cubed unsalted butter with pastry blender or two knives until mixture resembles coarse crumbs. Combine 3 tablespoons water and $\frac{1}{2}$ teaspoon cider vinegar in small bowl. Add to flour mixture; mix with fork until dough forms, adding additional water as needed. Form dough into disc; wrap in plastic wrap. Refrigerate 30 minutes.

Oat Streusel: Combine $\frac{1}{4}$ cup all-purpose flour, $\frac{1}{4}$ cup old-fashioned oats, $\frac{1}{4}$ cup granulated sugar, $\frac{1}{4}$ cup packed light brown sugar and $\frac{1}{8}$ teaspoon salt in medium bowl. Add $\frac{1}{4}$ cup ($\frac{1}{2}$ stick) cubed unsalted butter; crumble with fingertips until mixture resembles coarse crumbs.

plum & walnut pie

sweet potato pecan pie

1 unbaked deep-dish 9-inch pie crust
1½ cups pecan halves
½ cup light corn syrup
1 egg white
2 cups puréed cooked sweet potatoes
     (about 1½ pounds uncooked sweet potatoes)
⅓ cup packed brown sugar
1 teaspoon vanilla
½ teaspoon ground cinnamon
¼ teaspoon salt
   Pinch ground nutmeg
   Pinch ground cloves
2 eggs, beaten

1. Preheat oven to 400°F. Prick holes in bottom of crust with fork. Bake 10 minutes or until light brown. Cool completely on wire rack.

2. *Reduce oven temperature to 350°F.* Combine pecans, corn syrup and egg white in small bowl. Combine sweet potatoes, brown sugar, vanilla, cinnamon, salt, nutmeg and cloves in large bowl. Stir in eggs. Spread evenly in crust. Spoon pecan mixture evenly over top.

3. Bake 45 minutes or until filling is puffed and topping is golden brown. Cool completely on wire rack.   *Makes 8 servings*

sweet potato pecan pie

creamy vanilla apple pie

1 egg
6 to 8 apples, peeled and sliced ¼ inch thick
1 cup granulated sugar
1 cup vanilla yogurt
4 to 6 tablespoons all-purpose flour
1 teaspoon vanilla
½ teaspoon ground cinnamon
1 unbaked 9-inch pie crust
Spiced Crumb Topping (recipe follows)

1. Preheat oven to 350°F. Beat egg in medium bowl. Add apples, granulated sugar, yogurt, flour, vanilla and cinnamon; toss to coat. Spoon into crust.

2. Prepare Spiced Crumb Topping. Sprinkle over apple mixture.

3. Bake 1 hour or until topping is golden brown. Cool completely on wire rack.   *Makes 8 servings*

spiced crumb topping

1 cup all-purpose flour
½ cup granulated sugar
½ cup packed brown sugar
½ cup (1 stick) butter, melted
¼ teaspoon ground cinnamon

Combine all ingredients in medium bowl; stir until blended.

creamy vanilla apple pie

peanut butter cup pie

Chocolate Wafer Crust (recipe follows)
2/3 cup sugar
3 tablespoons cornstarch
1/2 teaspoon salt
2 1/2 cups whole milk
3 egg yolks, beaten
1/2 cup creamy peanut butter
1 teaspoon vanilla
2/3 cup chopped mini peanut butter cups
Chocolate Ganache (recipe follows)
Additional mini peanut butter cups (optional)

1. Preheat oven to 350°F. Prepare Chocolate Wafer Crust. Bake 5 minutes. Cool completely on wire rack.

2. Combine sugar, cornstarch and salt in large saucepan; stir in milk and egg yolks. Bring to a boil over medium heat; cook until thickened, stirring occasionally. Remove from heat; stir in peanut butter and vanilla until smooth. Transfer to medium bowl; cover and refrigerate 1 hour.

3. Stir chopped peanut butter cups into filling; spread evenly in crust. Cover and refrigerate 4 hours.

4. Prepare Chocolate Ganache. Let stand 15 minutes. Drizzle over pie. Garnish with additional peanut butter cups.   *Makes 8 servings*

Chocolate Wafer Crust: Break up 30 chocolate wafers and place in food processor. Add 1 1/2 tablespoons sugar. Process, pouring 1/2 cup (1 stick) melted unsalted butter through feed tube until well mixed. Press mixture on bottom and up side of 9-inch pie plate.

Chocolate Ganache: Bring 1/4 cup half-and-half to a boil in small heavy saucepan. Remove from heat; stir in 4 ounces finely chopped semisweet chocolate. Stir until chocolate is melted.

peanut butter cup pie

peach raspberry pie

Single-Crust Pie Pastry (recipe follows)
5 cups sliced peaches (about 2 pounds)
2 tablespoons lemon juice
1/2 pint raspberries
1/2 cup sugar
2 tablespoons quick-cooking tapioca
1/2 teaspoon ground cinnamon
1/4 teaspoon ground nutmeg
Almond Crumb Topping (recipe follows)
Whipped cream (optional)

1. Preheat oven to 400°F. Roll out pastry into 11-inch circle on floured surface. Line 9-inch pie plate with pastry; flute edge. Refrigerate 15 minutes.

2. Place peaches in large bowl. Sprinkle with lemon juice; toss to coat. Gently stir in raspberries.

3. Combine sugar, tapioca, cinnamon and nutmeg in small bowl. Sprinkle over fruit mixture; toss to coat. Spread evenly in crust. Prepare Almond Crumb Topping; sprinkle over pie.

4. Bake 15 minutes. *Reduce oven temperature to 350°F.* Bake 30 minutes or until bubbly. Cool 15 minutes on wire rack. Serve warm or at room temperature with whipped cream, if desired. *Makes 8 servings*

Single-Crust Pie Pastry: Combine 1¼ cups all-purpose flour and 1/2 teaspoon salt in medium bowl. Cut in 3 tablespoons shortening and 3 tablespoons cubed unsalted butter with pastry blender or two knives until mixture resembles coarse crumbs. Combine 3 tablespoons water and 1/2 teaspoon cider vinegar in small bowl. Add to flour mixture; mix with fork until dough forms, adding additional water as needed. Form dough into disc; wrap in plastic wrap. Refrigerate 30 minutes.

Almond Crumb Topping: Combine 2/3 cup old-fashioned or quick oats, 1/4 cup all-purpose flour, 1/4 cup packed brown sugar, 1/4 cup slivered almonds and 1/2 teaspoon ground cinnamon in medium bowl. Blend in 3 tablespoons softened unsalted butter until mixture resembles coarse crumbs.

peach raspberry pie

fruit and nut chocolate chip pie

2 eggs
½ cup packed brown sugar
¼ cup granulated sugar
1 teaspoon vanilla
½ teaspoon grated orange peel
⅛ teaspoon salt
1 cup (2 sticks) unsalted butter, melted and cooled
½ cup all-purpose flour
1 cup *each* semisweet chocolate chips, chopped pecans and raisins
1 unbaked 9-inch pie crust

1. Preheat oven to 325°F. Whisk eggs, brown sugar, granulated sugar, vanilla, orange peel and salt in large bowl. Whisk in butter and flour. Stir in chocolate chips, pecans and raisins. Spread evenly in crust.

2. Bake 50 minutes or until top is puffed and golden brown. Cool completely on wire rack.

Makes 10 servings

sweet 'n' spicy pecan pie

Prepared pie crust for one 9-inch pie
3 eggs
1 cup dark corn syrup
½ cup dark brown sugar
¼ cup (½ stick) butter or margarine, melted
1 tablespoon Original TABASCO® brand Pepper Sauce
1½ cups pecans, coarsely chopped

Preheat oven to 425°F. Place crust in 9-inch pie plate; flute edge of crust.

Beat eggs lightly in large bowl. Stir in corn syrup, brown sugar, butter and TABASCO® Sauce; mix well. Place pecans in prepared pie crust; pour filling over pecans. Bake 15 minutes.

Reduce oven to 350°F. Bake pie 40 minutes or until knife inserted 1 inch from edge comes out clean. Cool pie on wire rack.

Makes 8 servings

fruit and nut chocolate chip pie

almond custard pie

1½ cups all-purpose flour
½ cup plus 1 tablespoon granulated sugar, divided
½ teaspoon salt, divided
½ cup (1 stick) unsalted butter, melted
3 eggs
¼ teaspoon ground cinnamon
2 cups half-and-half
½ teaspoon almond extract
1 tablespoon butter
¾ cup sliced almonds
2 tablespoons packed dark brown sugar

1. Preheat oven to 425°F. Combine flour, 1 tablespoon granulated sugar and ¼ teaspoon salt in large bowl. Slowly pour in melted butter, stirring until dough forms.

2. Transfer dough to 9-inch pie pan; press onto bottom and up side, forming high rim. Place on rimmed baking sheet. Bake 5 minutes. (It is not necessary to weigh down crust.)

3. *Reduce oven temperature to 325°F.* Beat eggs in large bowl. Beat in remaining ½ cup granulated sugar, cinnamon and remaining ¼ teaspoon salt. Beat in half-and-half and almond extract.

4. Melt 1 tablespoon butter in medium skillet over medium heat. Add almonds; cook and stir 2 minutes or until golden brown. Remove from heat; cool slightly. Pour custard into crust. Spoon almonds over custard; sprinkle with brown sugar.

5. Bake 30 minutes or until set. Cool 30 minutes on wire rack. Serve at room temperature or refrigerate until chilled. *Makes 8 servings*

almond custard pie

walnut & maple syrup pie

1½ cups all-purpose flour
¾ teaspoon salt, divided
⅓ cup shortening
3 tablespoons unsalted butter, cubed
4 to 6 tablespoons ice water
3 eggs
1 cup maple syrup
6 tablespoons packed dark brown sugar
3 tablespoons unsalted butter, melted
¾ teaspoon vanilla
1½ cups coarsely chopped walnuts

1. Combine flour and ¼ teaspoon salt in medium bowl. Cut in shortening and cubed butter with pastry blender or two knives until mixture resembles coarse crumbs. Stir in water, 2 tablespoons at a time, until dough forms. Shape dough into disc; wrap in plastic wrap. Refrigerate 30 minutes.

2. Preheat oven to 425°F. Roll out pastry into 11-inch circle on floured surface. Line 9-inch pie pan with pastry; flute edge. Place pie pan on rimmed baking sheet. Bake 5 minutes. (It is not necessary to weigh down crust.)

3. Beat eggs in large bowl. Stir in maple syrup, brown sugar, melted butter, vanilla and remaining ½ teaspoon salt until well blended. Stir in walnuts. Pour into crust.

4. *Reduce oven temperature to 350°F.* Bake 45 minutes or until walnuts are golden brown and filling is slightly puffed. Check pie after 30 minutes and tent with foil, if necessary, to prevent walnuts from burning. Cool 30 minutes on wire rack. *Makes 8 servings*

walnut & maple syrup pie

nestlé® toll house® chocolate chip pie

2 eggs
½ cup all-purpose flour
½ cup granulated sugar
½ cup packed brown sugar
¾ cup (1½ sticks) butter, softened
1 cup (6 ounces) NESTLÉ® TOLL HOUSE® Semi-Sweet Chocolate Morsels
1 cup chopped nuts
1 *unbaked* 9-inch (4-cup volume) deep-dish pie shell*
Sweetened whipped cream or ice cream (optional)

If using frozen pie shell, use deep-dish style, thawed completely. Bake on baking sheet; increase baking time slightly.

PREHEAT oven to 325°F.

BEAT eggs in large mixer bowl on high speed until foamy. Beat in flour, granulated sugar and brown sugar. Beat in butter. Stir in morsels and nuts. Spoon into pie shell.

BAKE for 55 to 60 minutes or until knife inserted halfway between outside edge and center comes out clean. Cool on wire rack. Serve warm with whipped cream.   *Makes 8 servings*

nestlé® toll house® chocolate chip pie

frozen german sweet chocolate pie

- 1 package (4 ounces) BAKER'S® GERMAN'S® Sweet Baking Chocolate
- 1/3 cup milk, divided
- 4 ounces (1/2 of 8-ounce package) PHILADELPHIA® Cream Cheese, softened
- 2 tablespoons sugar
- 2 cups thawed COOL WHIP® Whipped Topping
- 1 HONEY MAID® Graham Pie Crust (6 ounces)

MICROWAVE chocolate and 2 tablespoons of the milk in large microwavable bowl on HIGH 1½ to 2 minutes or until chocolate is almost melted, stirring after each minute. Stir until chocolate is completely melted. Add cream cheese, sugar and remaining milk; beat with wire whisk until well blended. Refrigerate 10 minutes to cool.

ADD whipped topping. Stir gently until well blended. Spoon into crust.

FREEZE 4 hours or until firm. Let stand at room temperature or in refrigerator about 15 minutes or until pie can be cut easily. Top with chocolate curls before serving, if desired. Store leftover pie in freezer.

Makes 8 servings

Coconut Crust Variation: Heat oven to 350°F. Mix 1 package (7 ounces) BAKER'S® ANGEL FLAKE® Coconut (2⅔ cups) and 1/3 cup butter or margarine, melted. Press onto bottom and up sides of 9-inch pie plate. Bake 20 to 30 minutes or until golden brown. Cool on wire rack.

Prep Time: 20 minutes | Total Time: 4 hours 30 minutes (includes freezing)

amaretto coconut cream pie

¼ cup flaked coconut
1 container (8 ounces) whipped topping, divided
1 container (8 ounces) coconut cream or vanilla yogurt
¼ cup amaretto liqueur
1 package (4-serving size) coconut instant pudding and pie filling mix
1 (6-ounce) graham cracker pie crust
Fresh strawberries and mint leaves (optional)

1. Preheat oven to 350°F. Spread coconut in even layer on baking sheet. Bake 5 minutes or until golden brown, stirring frequently. Cool completely on wire rack.

2. Combine 2 cups whipped topping, yogurt and amaretto in large bowl. Add pudding mix; whisk 2 minutes or until thickened.

3. Spread pudding mixture evenly in crust; spread remaining whipped topping over filling. Sprinkle with toasted coconut. Garnish with strawberries and mint. Refrigerate 2 hours or until ready to serve.

Makes 8 servings

easy s'more pies

¾ cup sour cream
6 graham cracker mini pie crusts
¾ cup milk chocolate chips
1½ cups mini marshmallows

1. Spread 2 tablespoons sour cream evenly in each crust. Sprinkle with 2 tablespoons chocolate chips and ¼ cup marshmallows.

2. Preheat grill to medium-low. Place pies on grill; cover with 13×9-inch metal cake pan and grill 5 minutes or until marshmallows and chocolate are melted, checking frequently. Serve hot.

Makes 6 servings

amaretto coconut cream pie

crunchy ice cream pie

1 (8-ounce) chocolate bar, chopped
2 tablespoons butter
1½ cups crisp rice cereal
½ gallon chocolate chip or fudge ripple ice cream, softened
Hot fudge dessert topping

1. Spray 9-inch pie plate with nonstick cooking spray.

2. Combine chocolate and butter in top of double boiler over simmering water; cook and stir until chocolate is melted. Remove from heat. Add cereal; stir to coat. Transfer to prepared pie plate; press on bottom and up side to form crust.

3. Spread ice cream evenly in crust. Cover and freeze until ready to serve.

4. Let stand at room temperature 10 minutes before serving. Drizzle with dessert topping.

Makes 6 servings

egg custard pie

1 cup sugar
1 cup evaporated milk
2 eggs
1 teaspoon vanilla
1 unbaked 9-inch pie crust
1 teaspoon butter, cubed

Preheat oven to 325°F. Combine sugar, evaporated milk, eggs and vanilla in medium saucepan. Cook over high heat 2 minutes or until thickened, stirring constantly. Pour into crust. Dot with butter. Bake 40 minutes or until knife inserted into center comes out clean. Cool completely on wire rack.

Makes 8 servings

crunchy ice cream pie

carnation® key lime pie

- 1 can (14 ounces) NESTLÉ® CARNATION® Sweetened Condensed Milk
- 1/2 cup (about 3 medium limes) fresh lime juice
- 1 teaspoon grated lime peel
- 1 *prepared* 9-inch (6 ounces) graham cracker crumb crust
- 2 cups frozen whipped topping, thawed
  Lime peel twists or lime slices (optional)

BEAT sweetened condensed milk and lime juice in small mixer bowl until combined; stir in lime peel. Pour into crust; spread with whipped topping. Refrigerate for 2 hours or until set. Garnish with lime peel twists.

Makes 8 servings

mexican ice cream pie

- 1 cup butter pecan ice cream, softened
- 1 (6-ounce) chocolate crumb pie crust
- 3/4 cup caramel dessert topping
- 2 cups coffee ice cream, softened
- 1 jar (12 ounces) hot fudge dessert topping
- 1/2 cup coffee liqueur

1. Spread butter pecan ice cream evenly in crust. Freeze 20 minutes or until semi-firm.

2. Spread caramel topping over butter pecan ice cream. Freeze 20 minutes or until firm.

3. Spread coffee ice cream over caramel. Freeze pie 6 hours or overnight.

4. Combine hot fudge topping and coffee liqueur in small saucepan over medium heat; cook and stir until heated through.

5. Let stand at room temperature 10 minutes before serving. Drizzle with hot fudge mixture.

Makes 6 to 8 servings

carnation® key lime pie

oreo® ice cream shop pie

$\frac{1}{2}$ cup hot fudge dessert topping, divided
1 HONEY MAID® Graham Pie Crust (6 ounces)
1 tub (8 ounces) COOL WHIP® Whipped Topping, thawed, divided
$1\frac{1}{4}$ cups cold milk
2 packages (4-serving size each) JELL-O® OREO® Flavor Instant Pudding & Pie Filling

REMOVE 2 tablespoons of the fudge topping; set aside. Spoon remaining topping into crust; spread to evenly cover bottom of crust. Top with half of the whipped topping; freeze 10 minutes.

POUR milk into large bowl. Add dry pudding mixes. Beat with wire whisk 2 minutes or until well blended. (Mixture will be thick.) Gently stir in remaining whipped topping. Spoon over whipped topping layer in crust.

FREEZE 4 hours or until firm. Remove pie from freezer 15 minutes before serving. Let stand at room temperature to soften slightly. Drizzle with the reserved 2 tablespoons fudge topping. Store leftover pie in freezer.

Makes 10 servings

Variation: For more chocolate flavor, prepare as directed using an OREO® Pie Crust.

oreo® ice cream shop pie

pistachio ice cream pie

1 jar (12 ounces) hot fudge dessert topping, divided
1 (6-ounce) chocolate crumb pie crust
4 cups pistachio ice cream, softened
1/2 cup chopped pistachios

1. Spread half of dessert topping over bottom of crust; freeze 10 minutes. Spread ice cream evenly over dessert topping. Sprinkle with pistachios. Cover and freeze 2 hours or until firm.

2. Let stand at room temperature 10 minutes. Warm remaining dessert topping according to package directions; serve with pie.

Makes 8 servings

no bake peanut butter pie

4 ounces cream cheese
1 cup powdered sugar, sifted
1 cup crunchy peanut butter
1/2 cup milk
1 container (8 ounces) whipped topping
1 deep-dish graham cracker or chocolate-flavored crust

In large mixer bowl, combine cream cheese and powdered sugar; mix well. Add peanut butter and mix. Slowly add milk and mix well. Fold in whipped topping. Pour into pie crust and cover. Freeze for at least 30 minutes. If desired, drizzle each serving with chocolate syrup.

Makes 8 servings

*Favorite recipe from **Peanut Advisory Board***

pistachio ice cream pie

triple-layer lemon pie

   2 cups cold milk
   2 packages (4-serving size each) JELL-O® Lemon Flavor Instant
      Pudding & Pie Filling
   1 HONEY MAID® Graham Pie Crust (6 ounces)
   1 tub (8 ounces) COOL WHIP® Whipped Topping, thawed, divided
      Lemon peel, optional

POUR milk into large bowl. Add dry pudding mixes. Beat with wire whisk 2 minutes or until well blended. (Mixture will be thick.)

SPREAD 1½ cups of the pudding onto bottom of crust; set aside. Add half of the whipped topping to remaining pudding; stir gently until well blended. Spread over pudding layer in crust; top with the remaining whipped topping.

REFRIGERATE 3 hours or until set. Garnish with lemon peel, if desired. Store leftover pie in refrigerator. *Makes 8 servings*

fresh cantaloupe pie

   1 cantaloupe, peeled, seeded and cut into bite-size pieces
   1 cup sugar
   1 tablespoon vanilla
   1 (6-ounce) graham cracker pie crust
   1 container (8 ounces) whipped topping

Place cantaloupe in medium saucepan; cover with water. Bring to a boil over high heat. Reduce heat to low; simmer until tender. Drain well. Stir in sugar and vanilla. Spread evenly in crust. Top with whipped topping. *Makes 8 servings*

triple-layer lemon pie

banana split pie

- 2 cups cold milk
- 2 packages (4-serving size each) JELL-O® Vanilla Flavor Instant Pudding & Pie Filling
- 1 HONEY MAID® Graham Pie Crust (6 ounces)
- 1 cup sliced fresh strawberries, divided
- 1 banana, sliced
- 1 tub (8 ounces) COOL WHIP® Whipped Topping, thawed, divided

POUR milk into large bowl. Add dry pudding mixes. Beat with wire whisk 2 minutes. Spread 1½ cups of the pudding onto bottom of crust.

TOP with half of the strawberries; cover with bananas. Add half of the whipped topping to remaining pudding; stir gently until well blended. Spread over fruit layer in crust.

SPREAD remaining whipped topping over pie to within 1 inch of crust. Top with remaining strawberries.

REFRIGERATE 3 hours or until set. Store leftovers in refrigerator.

Makes 8 servings

Jazz It Up: Garnish with ¼ cup PLANTER'S® Pecan Pieces and chocolate syrup just before serving.

Prep Time: 15 minutes (plus refrigerating)

banana split pie

chocolate peanut butter pie

1 can (14 ounces) sweetened condensed milk
¼ cup creamy peanut butter
2 tablespoons unsweetened cocoa powder
1 container (8 ounces) whipped topping
1 (6-ounce) chocolate crumb pie crust

1. Beat sweetened condensed milk, peanut butter and cocoa in large bowl with electric mixer at medium speed until smooth and well blended. Fold in whipped topping. Pour mixture into crust.

2. Freeze 6 hours or overnight. Let stand at room temperature 10 minutes before serving.   *Makes 8 servings*

coconut cream pie

1½ cups sweetened shredded coconut
8 containers (about 3 ounces each) vanilla pudding
1 (6-ounce) graham cracker pie crust

1. Preheat oven to 350°F. Spread coconut on baking sheet. Toast coconut 5 minutes, stirring frequently. Cool completely on wire rack. Reserve 2 tablespoons coconut.

2. Combine pudding and remaining coconut in medium bowl.

3. Spread pudding mixture evenly in crust. Sprinkle reserved coconut over top. Refrigerate 1 hour or until set.   *Makes 8 servings*

chocolate peanut butter pie

grasshopper pudding pie

    4 FAMOUS® Chocolate Wafers, divided
 1½ cups cold fat-free milk
  ¼ teaspoon peppermint extract
    1 package (4-serving size) JELL-O® Pistachio Flavor Fat Free
        Sugar Free Instant Pudding & Pie Filling
    2 cups thawed COOL WHIP® Sugar Free Whipped Topping
    1 square BAKER'S® Semi-Sweet Chocolate, chopped

CRUSH 2 wafers; sprinkle onto bottom of 9-inch pie plate sprayed with cooking spray.

BEAT milk, extract and pudding mix with whisk 2 minutes. Stir in whipped topping and chopped chocolate; spread into pie plate. Top with remaining wafers, cut into quarters.

FREEZE 6 hours or until firm. Remove pie from freezer 10 minutes before serving; let stand at room temperature to soften slightly before cutting to serve. *Makes 8 servings*

very strawberry pie

    1 container (8 ounces) strawberry cream cheese
    4 containers (about 3 ounces each) vanilla pudding
    2 tablespoons strawberry dessert topping
    1 (6-ounce) chocolate crumb pie crust
    1 pint strawberries, hulled and sliced

1. Beat cream cheese in medium bowl with electric mixer at low speed 30 seconds or until smooth. Add pudding and dessert topping; beat 1 minute or until blended.

2. Pour mixture into crust. Refrigerate 10 minutes. Arrange strawberries on top of pie. *Makes 6 servings*

Serving Suggestion: For a special touch, drizzle top of pie with strawberry or chocolate dessert topping just before serving.

grasshopper pudding pie

chocolate cookie pie

1 cup whipping cream
20 chocolate sandwich cookies
1 (6-ounce) chocolate crumb pie crust

1. Beat cream in large bowl with electric mixer at high speed until soft peaks form. Place 14 cookies in resealable food storage bag and crush into coarse crumbs with rolling pin or mallet.

2. Stir crumbs into whipped cream; spread evenly in crust. Garnish with remaining cookies. Cover and freeze until ready to serve. Let stand at room temperature 10 minutes before serving. *Makes 8 servings*

easy cherry cream pie

1 pint vanilla ice cream, softened
½ (16-ounce) package frozen dark sweet cherries, chopped
1 cup whipping cream
1 tablespoon powdered sugar
⅛ teaspoon almond extract
1 (6-ounce) chocolate crumb or graham cracker pie crust

1. Combine ice cream and cherries in large bowl just until blended.

2. Beat cream, powdered sugar and almond extract in medium bowl with electric mixer at medium speed until soft peaks form.

3. Spread ice cream evenly in crust. Spoon whipped cream evenly on top. Freeze 1 hour or until firm. Let stand at room temperature 10 minutes before serving. *Makes 8 servings*

Prep Time: 10 minutes

chocolate cookie pie

banana cream pie with caramel drizzle

1½ bananas
 1 HONEY MAID® Graham Pie Crust (6 ounces)
 2 cups cold milk
 2 packages (4-serving size each) JELL-O® Vanilla Flavor Instant
    Pudding & Pie Filling
 2 cups thawed COOL WHIP® French Vanilla Whipped Topping,
    divided
 ¼ cup caramel dessert topping

ARRANGE 1 sliced banana on bottom of crust.

POUR milk into large bowl. Add dry pudding mixes. Beat with wire whisk 2 minutes or until well blended. Gently stir in 1 cup of the whipped topping; spoon into crust.

REFRIGERATE 4 hours or until set. Drizzle with caramel topping just before serving. Top with remaining half banana, sliced, and 1 cup whipped topping. Store leftovers in refrigerator. *Makes 10 servings*

Variation: Prepare as directed, using JELL-O® Banana Cream Flavor Instant Pudding & Pie Filling.

Prep Time: 15 minutes (plus refrigerating)

The publisher would like to thank the companies and organizations listed below for the use of their recipes and photographs in this publication.

Campbell Soup Company

Dole Food Company, Inc.

Duncan Hines® and Moist Deluxe® are registered trademarks of Pinnacle Foods Corp.

The Hershey Company

Kraft Foods Global, Inc.

McIlhenny Company (TABASCO® brand Pepper Sauce)

Nestlé USA

Ortega®, A Division of B&G Foods, Inc.

Peanut Advisory Board

Banana Cream Pie with Caramel
   Drizzle, 138
Banana Split Pie, 130
Black Bottom Banana Cream Pie,
   84
Ginger Cream Banana Pie, 87
Blackberry Custard Pie, 56
Black Bottom Banana Cream Pie,
   84

Blueberry
   Blueberry Pie, 38
   Enlightened Fresh Triple-Berry
      Pie, 42
   Summer Berry Pie, 64
Brown Sugar Meringue, 87
Brown Sugar Streusel Topping, 94
Buttermilk Pie, 26
Butter Pecan Pie, 17

C
Caribbean Coconut Pie, 18
Carnation® Key Lime Pie, 122
Celia's Flat Fruit Pie, 60
Cheddar Streusel, 16

Cherry
   Apple & Cherry Pie, 46
   Easy Cherry Cream Pie, 136
   Peach Cherry Pie, 94
Chilly Lemon Pie, 76

Chocolate
   Black Bottom Banana Cream Pie,
      84
   Chocolate & Peanut Pie, 96
   Chocolate and Vanilla-Swirled
      Cheese Pie, 88
   Chocolate Caramel Surprise
      Pie, 14
   Chocolate Chess Pie, 8
   Chocolate Cookie Pie, 136
   Chocolate Ganache, 104
   Chocolate Mint Cookie Pie, 72
   Chocolate Peanut Butter Pie,
      132
   Chocolate Velvet Pie, 68
   Chocolate Wafer Crust, 104
   Crunchy Ice Cream Pie, 120
   Easy Cherry Cream Pie, 136
   Easy S'more Pies, 118
   Fancy Fudge Pie, 20
   Frozen German Sweet
      Chocolate Pie, 116
   Fruit and Nut Chocolate Chip
      Pie, 108
   Granny's No-Crust Chocolate
      Pie, 82
   Grasshopper Pudding Pie, 134
   Kansas City Mud Pie, 24
   Mexican Ice Cream Pie, 122

METRIC CONVERSION CHART

VOLUME MEASUREMENTS (dry)

$1/8$ teaspoon = 0.5 mL
$1/4$ teaspoon = 1 mL
$1/2$ teaspoon = 2 mL
$3/4$ teaspoon = 4 mL
1 teaspoon = 5 mL
1 tablespoon = 15 mL
2 tablespoons = 30 mL
$1/4$ cup = 60 mL
$1/3$ cup = 75 mL
$1/2$ cup = 125 mL
$2/3$ cup = 150 mL
$3/4$ cup = 175 mL
1 cup = 250 mL
2 cups = 1 pint = 500 mL
3 cups = 750 mL
4 cups = 1 quart = 1 L

VOLUME MEASUREMENTS (fluid)

1 fluid ounce (2 tablespoons) = 30 mL
4 fluid ounces ($1/2$ cup) = 125 mL
8 fluid ounces (1 cup) = 250 mL
12 fluid ounces ($1 1/2$ cups) = 375 mL
16 fluid ounces (2 cups) = 500 mL

WEIGHTS (mass)

$1/2$ ounce = 15 g
1 ounce = 30 g
3 ounces = 90 g
4 ounces = 120 g
8 ounces = 225 g
10 ounces = 285 g
12 ounces = 360 g
16 ounces = 1 pound = 450 g

DIMENSIONS

$1/16$ inch = 2 mm
$1/8$ inch = 3 mm
$1/4$ inch = 6 mm
$1/2$ inch = 1.5 cm
$3/4$ inch = 2 cm
1 inch = 2.5 cm

OVEN TEMPERATURES

250°F = 120°C
275°F = 140°C
300°F = 150°C
325°F = 160°C
350°F = 180°C
375°F = 190°C
400°F = 200°C
425°F = 220°C
450°F = 230°C

BAKING PAN SIZES

Utensil	Size in Inches/Quarts	Metric Volume	Size in Centimeters
Baking or Cake Pan (square or rectangular)	8×8×2	2 L	20×20×5
	9×9×2	2.5 L	23×23×5
	12×8×2	3 L	30×20×5
	13×9×2	3.5 L	33×23×5
Loaf Pan	8×4×3	1.5 L	20×10×7
	9×5×3	2 L	23×13×7
Round Layer Cake Pan	8×1½	1.2 L	20×4
	9×1½	1.5 L	23×4
Pie Plate	8×1¼	750 mL	20×3
	9×1¼	1 L	23×3
Baking Dish or Casserole	1 quart	1 L	—
	1½ quart	1.5 L	—
	2 quart	2 L	—